T0146433

Inspirations *from the* Heart

MARILYN SANDBERG GRENAT

INSPIRATIONS FROM THE HEART

*All Scriptures are taken from the Holy Bible, New International Version®.
NIV®. Copyright © 1973, 1978, 1984 by International Bible Society.
Used by permission of Zondervan. All rights reserved. [Biblica]*

iUniverse books may be ordered through booksellers or by contacting:

*iUniverse
1663 Liberty Drive
Bloomington, IN 47403
www.iuniverse.com
1-800-Authors (1-800-288-4677)*

*ISBN: 978-1-5320-5042-8 (sc)
ISBN: 978-1-5320-5043-5 (hc)
ISBN: 978-1-5320-5041-1 (e)*

Library of Congress Control Number: 2018907532

Print information available on the last page.

iUniverse rev. date: 07/12/2018

Dedication

I dedicate this book to my beloved husband,
Gene Grenat, deceased April 2, 2011.

My beloved son, Jeffrey Fleeger, deceased November 26, 2016.

My beloved daughter, Annette Fleeger Smith

My beloved daughter, Kristina Fleeger Oswalt,

My beloved daughter, Jennifer Fleeger Delong and

My beloved daughter-in-law, Joanna Fleeger

By Marilyn Sandberg Grenat

Acknowledgements

I want to thank my friends who encouraged me and listened to some previews of a few poems before they went to the publisher. I also am so appreciative of my publishing consultant, Josh Wales, that helped convert my format to the publisher's readability. He was so encouraging from the beginning and gave me constructive criticism and support.

The knowledgeable, scholar, Lawrence Mykitiuk, that agreed to write my foreword, has been my friend for several years. He is the Assistant Professor of Library Science at Purdue University Libraries, and has spoken at many symposiums and conferences, and is the author of several papers and a book. I am deeply grateful for his taking time out of his busy schedule to write the foreword for my book.

My family have also been encouraging and helpful. Thank you one and all; it means a great deal to me.

Table of Contents

Epigraph/Purpose

One of the greatest needs in the world is to find God's plan for your life and then let Him help you fullfill it. We are to serve others and show our love in our service that honors God.

NIV scripture: Colossians 3:23

"Whatever you do, work at it with all your heart, and working for the Lord, not for man."

Foreword

I feel honored to write about Marilyn Grenat as the author of the poetry in this book, because it comes from a heart of love and compassion.

My wife and I have come to know Marilyn through our involvement in the same church and in it, the same small group. There we have often benefited from her prayers and encouraging comments. We have known her since the time when both her wonderful husband Gene and her dear son Jeff were living. Both are now with the Lord. Having observed her absorb those losses and continue to give compassionate care to people who need her, especially those with physical needs, I am impressed with her resilience and her ability to lean on the Lord and on his community for comfort. Ultimately her strength is revealed in the unfailing vigor and sensitivity with which she embraces the life God gives her.

I feel sure that Marilyn's poems are another expression of the same caring outlook that motivates her in the rest of her life.

In a much earlier experience elsewhere, a church member announced that he was going to show slides of the Holy Land that evening. Much to the congregation's amusement, his Sunday morning preview opened with an attractive slide of the harbor at *Stockholm*! As a grateful, proud American who never slights any other group, Marilyn's loyalty to her Swedish relatives and ancestry are a model of pride in her heritage. Above all, she knows who she is, because she knows that spiritually, she belongs to the One who bought her.

Lawrence Mykytiuk
Associate Professor of Library Science
Purdue University
April 14, 2018

Introduction

I have read in the Reader's Digest that James W. Pennebaker, a Psychology Professor, at the University of Texas, said we should free write for twenty minutes a day to write our pain away. He said people who engage in expressive writing report feeling happier and less negative than they felt before.

I learned this myself before I ever read these words and I must agree that expressing your feelings on paper gives you a feeling of relaxation and release from your trauma.

It's been known that nearly 40% of folks who kept their traumas or grief to themselves went to the physicians more often than those who openly talked about them.

As things impress or depress me, I have found solace in expressing my feelings on paper. These writings ended up being in poem form. Over the years my little writings and readings have been shoved into a box. As I have recently lost my dear husband of twenty beautiful years, I am finding joy and comfort in re-reading and actually creating new ones.

I have joined them together again in one little journal. This little book is a combination of some other authors' inspirations along with many of my own writings. Those of others are documented, while all others are mine. I am encouraging other folks to journal their feelings.

Since I started this little journal in 2013, I have also lost my only son to cancer in 2016. Since this is a conglomeration of several years of poems, I have dated them and added some more recently after loosing him too. I lost my mother forty-nine years ago and penned my first little poem about her soon after she passed. She had a habit of always asking, "How are ya?" Being Swedish, we all love our coffee and the coffee pot was always on. Knowing these things about my mother, you will understand my simple poem of her.

I am a mother, grandmother, great grandmother, sister, daughter, aunt and mother-in-law who loves all of my family, so I have tried to express to each of them how important and how loved they are by me. I also was a wife. I told them that not one of them is loved more deeply than the other, but each is loved completely for their own individual assets and attributes just as though they were the only ones in my life. I would like to express to my readers how important it is to let their family members know how much they love them and how special they are.

Since my husband had alzheimer's and my son had cancer, I have written about those horrible diseases as well. I am now a caregiver for several who want to stay out of a nursing home and live in the comfort of their own homes. It is not only cheaper, but they usually thrive more efficiently at home.

The Lord has been gracious to me to allow me enough strength and health every day to perform these duties, and I feel blessed to be afforded this privilege and opportunity to serve others in this way.

We all grieve differently at different paces. Some take a few weeks, some take months, while others may take years. No one should tell another how to grieve or how long it should take. We should all go at our own pace, but not try to do it alone. If you need an understanding dear friend, a pastor or counselor to hear you out, then use them.

If you can relieve some of that tension by expressing yourself on paper, then do that. I know this procedure was a godsend for me and very therapeutic.

We have a trained group in our church called "Stephen Ministers" that have helped one-on-one many who are going through trauma. They don't "judge" or "tell" you what to do, but give you support, love, and are a sounding board.

Through my care giving, I always try to have a ready ear, as most folks just need to be heard and one with a loving, caring heart.

Perhaps others can relate or recall their own joys, memories, or traumas of days gone by or presently going through. I hope through sharing some of my experiences in my poems, you may find some solace or perhaps a smile or two in reading them. I have found this verse from the Bible to be true and uplifting.

Phillipians 4:13 "I can do all things through Christ which strengtheneth me." (NIV)

May God bless you in your journey/
Marilyn Sandberg Grenat

Other Quotes of Importance

"TO SUCCEED" by Ralph Waldo Emerson

"To win the respect of intelligent people, and the affection of children;
To appreciate beauty;
To find the best in others;
To leave the world a bit better;
To know that even one life has breathed easier because you lived.
This is to have succeeded."

"KINDNESS" by Mark Twain

"Kindness is the language which the deaf
can hear and the blind can see."

"WISDOM" by Albert Einstein and Don Quixote

"The more I learn, the more I realize I don't know."

"BE YOU" by Francis de Sales

"Do not wish to be anything but what or who you are,
And try to be that perfectly."

Religious

"Anger" James 1:19 from NIV/Bible

"Let every man be swift to hear, slow to anger, slow to wrath."

"Patience" I Thessalonians 5:14 from NIV/Bible

"Be patient toward all men."

"Harmony" I Peter 3:8 from NIV/Bible

"Live in harmony with one another, be sympathetic, love as brothers, be compassionate and humble."

"Goals" Phillipians 3:14 from NIV/Bible

"I press toward the mark for the prize of the high calling of God in Christ Jesus."

This is my prayer for my children and each of you. By Marilyn Sandberg Grenat

May my children remember our Heavenly Father's eternal goals for them as they live their lives from day to day, and then they will be fulfilling His plan and purpose for each of their lives. Lord God, may we all set our sights on the goal you have set for each of us, as it is more whole, complete, and beautiful than anything we could imagine for ourselves. I know you have designed a purpose for each of your created lovely individuals.

"Work" inspired by Colossians 3:23

"Whatever you do, work at it with all your heart, as working for the Lord, Not for man."

You can glorify God through your labor in the way you do it willingly with good humor and to the best of your ability. Use your gifts and talents for yourself and others. Your positive attitude, noticed by your coworkers that can influence their relationship to work. In these ways and more, you glorify God through your labor.

"What is a mother?"   By Helen Steiner Rice

It takes a mother's love to make a house a home,
It takes a mother's kindness to forgive us no matter how we roam.

It takes a mother's patience to bring a child up right,
And her courage and her cheerfulness to make a dark day bright.

It takes a mother's wisdom to recognize our needs,
And to give us reassurance by her loving words and deeds.

And that is why in all this world there could not be another
Who could fulfill God's purpose as completely as a mother.

For Mother "When we go home" *Deceased; June 18, 1969*
January 14, 1970

Our mother has gone before us—
Just as our Lord has done.
To prepare a place for us—
Leaving us in want of none.

I can picture her hustling about,
When she thinks we'll soon be
allowed,
To enter that pearly gate
Of that mansion so great.

She'll fuss and be so glad
To think that we'll soon be clad
In those lovely white gowns
That we may gladly wear around the grounds.

She'll meet us at the gate
With a smile so great.
And say, I'm sure, "How are ya?"
And we'll know we are home.

The coffee pot she'll probably have on,
And we'll all enjoy a cup at dawn.
And we'll know we are home.

"Mom is sitting there"   September, 2010

Sometimes with movement of a rocking chair,
I often think of Mom sitting there.

Occasionally the swing will swing,
And I think maybe she came on wing.

If anyone could be angelic and sing,
I know it'd be her with a zing.

Sometimes I talk to her as if she were there,
And then she answers with a stare.

Our mommas are always with us,
Because we wish it like a trust.

Her picture always smiles at me,
And I talk about her to grandchildren on my knee.

Even though they've never seen her,
I want them to know and concur,
That she is as special as finest fur.

Her legacy left to each,
Will prove she's a peach.

Mother's not gone, but she lives in all of us.
We talk with, think about, and praise our mom,
So you'll never forget how wonderful she was.

Our Father was born in Sweden,
But he came to America where we wanted to keep him.
He loved his new country and married a native named Helen.

He accomplished great deals,
Started a business, while Helen made meals.

A family was started,
And then they departed,
For a trip abroad.
All who knew Leonard, gave him applaud.

Many trips followed in the next few years
as were allowed.
Then heaven called Helen home,
And Leonard found Anna to roam.

They loved Sweden too,
And made trips anew.

It had always been summertime,
But now they wanted to visit the Christmas pine.

So then Leonard, Anna, and Marilyn-the three,
Left to visit relatives by the sea.

A beautiful time was had by all,
Until we saw the fall.

Unfortunately, Leonard had a heart attack,
That turned our trip completely back.

The next six weeks,
Brought rest and healing to peaks.

Len and Anna finally came home,
To see doctors who checked him with a fine-toothed comb.

Many family members came,
To welcome him without pain.
,
And wanted him to be up to par.

Daddy couldn't speak well,
But he was just happy we could sit a spell.

The good Lord thought he needed more rest,
So He decided to take the best.

Daddy joined our mother in the sky,
And poor Anna was left to cry.

We all would miss him a bunch,
And this created a nasty crunch.

Our dad was special in may ways,
And it would be very hard in future days.

While we're only here on loan,
We were grateful our daddy finally made it home.

"Big Brother, Ralph"

Having a big brother was special
To Marilyn, the little sister.

Ralph was three and a half years her senior,
That made him quite the mister.

Peoria was our home town,
where we started to put our roots down.

Then one year we all went to Sweden,
To Dad's family so we could meet 'em.

Ralph's typical display of disgust,
Was usually done in robust.

But when he thought little sister didn't
know,
It was only all for show.

At night when he was asleep,
In his room she would creep.

A kiss on his forehead she would plant,
But when awake was always scant.

One day she could hear
Him say to buddies not to bother his little sister.

High school friends they often shared,
For often to our house they came and cared.

Our mother made yummy pizzas,
And our friends enjoyed spending time in our home.

Our parents were fun,
And the kids spent time there on the run.

Ralph and our father would always give me a tease-
I think their male egos they felt must be appeased.

When it was time for Ralph to go off to college,
I felt like our family fell apart,
Even though he needed the knowledge.

Two years went fast and then off to the Army he went-
Then overseas he was soon sent.

He found his bride, Kathy, in Taiwan,
And brought her home to surprise the family.

And it wasn't long before we were blessed with baby Jackie.
Back to college for more education,
Ralph decided was the best for revelation.

Real Estate became their scheme,
And they did it as a team.
Chicago and Florida became their theme.

Happy they are planted way down there.
I just want you to be aware,

That your sister has always been happy
To have a good big brother that's pretty snappy!

"Thankfulness"

I want to thank all of my family for the wonderful memories you have given me. cherish memories of my children discovering the world around them and growing into womanhood and manhood, with all their cute antics and discoveries along the way.

This is why I have written a poem about each of you to show you how much you mean to me.

It's also been wonderful to have been born into a Christian family with a mother and a father that taught me right from wrong and gave me all the love an individual could ever want. They didn't send me to church; they TOOK me to church where we practiced love both with Christian friends and family as well as at home.

I was fortunate enough to have a good big brother who always had my back and allowed me to be in his life in a caring loving way.

As life has gone on, I was blessed with good Christian friends in Sunday School, Covenant Harbor Bible Camp in Wisconsin, and our denominational college at North Park College in Chicago. All of these wonderful places afforded me good Christian growth. Today my growth in God has been because I have been blessed with good leadership in our Evangelical Covenant Church. Thank you good friends for all my life experiences have given me.

"Early Love"

Early on in our dating starting in July of 1990, Gene made my heart stand still. We fell in love very quickly and at our age we knew what the epitome of good was. He was the perfect man in my eyes and I was the perfect woman in his eyes.

We don't always get to choose who we fall in love with, but we know it when it hits us square in the mind, heart, body and soul. Some times one loves the other more than they love the other party. It was equally a mutual admiration that makes for an easier smooth relationship. We did not have many difficulties to overcome.

They say "love is blind". Maybe it is to some degree. In the beginning, we ex-changed many cards and letters of love expressions.

Ecclesiastes 3:1 NIV/Bible says, "To everything there is a season, and a time to every purpose under the heaven." This was our season to be happy. We had both been married before and had had our children, and we were in our fifties.

Marilyn Sandberg Fleeger had been introduced to Bernard Eugene (Gene) Grenat in July, 1990 by Marilyn's sister-in-law, Kathy, who was my brother's wife. Ralph and Gene had graduated from Jefferson High School in 1955, and were sitting at the same table for their thirty-fifth high school reunion dinner. Upon finding out that Gene was looking for a nice Christian girl in Lafayette, Kathy moved on it. He had come back recently from working in California the last twenty plus years as an avionics electronics technician. She said to Gene, "I have just the girl for you," with Marilyn in mind. After giving him my phone number, he looked me up in the school yearbook, and claimed he remembered who I was. He told his mom, "She's that cute little freshman while I was a senior."

The first time, a couple of days later, he called me and we talked for about an hour. He had such a smooth, deep, sexy voice, and I was impressed with his fun-sounding yet intelligent conversation.

In a couple more days, he called and we talked for about three hours with even more intrigue. Could it be there was finally a man who did not lack for intelligent conversation and who could outtalk me?!

Nearly three weeks after we met and dated, I was having my fiftieth birth- day and working in Accounting at Purdue University. I had been a single mother for nearly thirteen years, rearing four children on my own.

My only son had just graduated from my Alma Mater, North Park University, in Chicago, Il., and had landed a job with Delta Airlines as a reservationist. He plan- ned to fly me with him to Hawaii for my fiftieth birthday celebration for ten days.

We had quite a trip planned. Meeting Gene and planning such a trip, I felt like my life was just beginning!

Gene's card to me on my fiftieth read, "Don't worry about fifty, that just means you're five times better than ten!"

The next ten days for Jeff and me were glorious as we drove around two islands, and filled our days and nights with beautiful sights and events.

Meanwhile, back home, poor Gene paced the floor endlessly doing as many odd jobs as his mother could find for him to do. She said later that she knew he was in love and hooked when he moped around every day waiting for my return. He got more cards for me to welcome me back home and even wrote me a poem about how he had been waiting.

Wow! Gene could hardly wait until my return, and then he got to meet my son, Jeff, for the first time. He swept me into his arms and lifted me off the floor a whole foot as he was 6'2" to my 5'1". He twirled me around and kissed me long and hard before even saying a word. Then he almost cried as he said, "I've missed you so much, I couldn't stand it!" His card read:

> "I can't eat
> I can't sleep
> I can't think...
> Of anything but you.

Welcome back!!!

> The surest signs of love-almost as sure as a single, long-stemmed rose.*

Love, Gene"

*This had become our expression of love early on.
A long-stemmed red rose means love and it became our symbol.

This is a copy of the beautiful poem Gene wrote in his own words and penmanship, which he included in the "arrival" card.

"I am waiting" by Gene Grenat   *September 12,1990*

(Poem of love for Marilyn)

For a niche in your armor to
Appear and say your are less than
Angelic and are still a struggling mortal.

For the first time my mind and body are not
Willing to leave all other interests behind and
Rush to be with you under any pretext.

For the feeling to hug and kiss you
At all times I am with you, to
Become less than desperate.

For this state of awe to be
Replaced with a knowledge
My prayers for a wonderful
Mate have been answered.
For proof Male and Female
True Virgos can't be <u>Perfect</u>
Marriage partners as well.

For this string of absolutely
Astounding sameness of feelings
And views to end and indicate a
Less than amazing agreement
Between us.

For you to have a great time in
Hawaii with Jeff and return
With a sense of missing me.

Lovingly,
Gene

"Cards"

Another loving card read: September 26, 1990

"I love being us
I feel closer to you now than I ever felt before…
There is something wonderful
Knowing that we've made a choice to be together, to be a pair,
You and I….a pair.

I like the way that sounds–
The oneness, the unity it represents.
I love being us…
Being so much a part of each other
That one cannot be separated
From the other.

How can one take away the waves from the ocean,
The stars from the night…
Or you from me and have them ever be the same?

You and I were always meant to be together."

Then he said, "I couldn't say it better myself.
        I love you…" Gene

We got married on December 22, 1990, and the snow came down so hard that evening

That we worried about people getting home safely. We couldn't leave on our honeymoon for several days. I was exhausted from helping to plan my daughter's wedding the week before, doing all the Christmas shopping and baking, and then our wedding. I was happy to relax a bit. This still was a beautiful time for a wedding, and many people were home or around to share it with us.

Gene sent me this card on our first month anniversary January 22, 1991

It read:

"I love being with you.

I love all the joy that having you in my life brings to me.

From our most intimate moments alone to the pride I feel in you.

When we're out somewhere together, I love all that we share,

I love the laughter, the understanding, and the fact that so much about us-

Our minds, our bodies, our hearts, our feelings—

Should touch so closely and perfectly together

Most of all, I love you, and that special, gentle way you have-

That sensitive and loving side of you

That you save just for me when we're alone together."

He added: 'Honey: sometimes I love it tooo much.

All my love, Gene'

On Gene's first Father's Day with me, I gave him this card: June 16, 1991.

"I love you for so many reasons.

I love you for all the special qualities that make you "you", one of a kind,

The only one in the world for me.

I love you for the things you say that bring such special meaning to my life,

And I love you for the silent times when your eyes and your arms tell me all

I want to know.

I love thinking of all the adventures we may share, the places we may go, the

Discoveries we may make together.

I love you for so many reasons, and all of them are wonderful."

Happy Father's Day!

With all my love, Marilyn

We had twenty beautiful married years together, and they were beautiful even though he had Alzheimer's for eleven years. He was such a brilliant man, and it was hard to see him lose his memory. He could remember some memories from long ago after I made him a special photo album to help trigger those memories, but his short term memory loss was difficult to cope with at times. Even though he forgot names, he still was able to look at me with love in his eyes. Alzheimer patients respond to loving touches, smiles and gentle talk. I know his love still came through when he forgot he was married to me, but liked me so much that he asked me to marry him. He had enough wits about him to know he cared for me. So sweet.

I said, "Sweetie, that's very flattering, but we are already married." Then he said, "Oh, good!"

The moment you walked through my front door, you had me from the start.
That tall, dark, handsome figure with a smile that could melt any heart.

It matched your deep, soothing, sexy voice that I had heard on the phone
several times prior.
Now they were all together, and I knew my sister-in-law was no liar.

She said we were a match,
And it was beginning to feel you were a catch.

This six foot two frame,
With a beautiful violet in hand you came.

It was so sweet and precious-I almost cried-
For that was my favorite flower.
How could you have known?
I had on my lavender dress, and
That was your favorite color.
How could I have known?

We had only talked twice on the phone,
Fate was at work here and early fond memories were already forming.

For later we discovered,
These trivial things were uncovered.

Gene took me to a very nice restaurant for dinner,
And we both ordered spaghetti-what a winner!

We found we had the same tastes in food as well.
This would surely make it all jell.

Everyone grew to admire my Gene, and with initials G.G., he acquired
the name of "Gentle Giant".

His tall stature made him a giant, but large he was in many qualities.
Gentle as well were his assets,
At which I can truly attest.

Now that you're gone, I remember them well,
And relive the memories that were so swell.

My sweet Gentle Giant how I long for the touch of your hand;
It was the sweetest in all the land.

You had a special way of touching my chin-
That always made me grin.

You would gaze into my eyes with love, and my heart would melt.
Your tender sweet kiss,
Would give me such bliss.

How could this sweet Gentle Giant be so swift,
To give my heart such a lift?

Because he really was my Gentle Giant,
And I miss him beyond all words or imagination.

It's almost been three months;
Perhaps I'll get over the humps.

I surely do hope so, because my dear sweet Gentle Giant, I miss you so.

I'll see you again my precious one,
In that great new land where you've already gone.

    Lovingly, your Marilyn

"Flowers for Gene"

My beautiful Christmas amaryllis
Bloomed the day Gene died.

It was a sign, I believe,
To comfort and retrieve.

A freshness of beauty and lasting life;
It gave me a feeling of no strife.

His white tulips on his casket, also
Rose up to the occasion-
To bring us joy and happiness and a time to praise Him.

I felt the Lord had
Commanded the flowers to take away the bad.

It caused me to smile,
And pause a while.

"A year has passed"   *April 2, 2012*

Months have grown day by day;
It's now a year since you have gone away.

Thoughts are full and hearts do weigh,
Without you here to share the way.

Time may dull the hand of fate;
Memory forever recalls the date.

Secret tears and loving thoughts
Will be with me forever caught.

Gone are the days we used share,
But in our hearts you're always there.

Never more than a thought away,
Loved and remembered every day.

Wait for me, I will see you again.

    Your loving wife, Marilyn

My Children

"Annette Yvonne" (my firstborn)

(black & white wedding photo of Annette & Dave-RFR-120312)

What a glorious day, the day I discovered
That I should have my first baby uncovered.

I couldn't believe my calendar day counting,
When I realized my joy was mounting.

Her daddy and I were living
in San Diego,
And her dad was a sailor at
sea, where he loved to go.

I was told I could transfer to
the office of GMAC;
I was an accounting
representative, don't you see!

Lee had a year left to serve,
And I left Chicago with lots
of nerve.

We married in August,
With hopes to enjoy a new location with robust!

It was hard to keep Lee out of toy stores;
He wanted to buy everything for his new child on the floors.

Of course my husband was aboard ship,
The day I went to submit.

I drove myself to the doctor's office for my examination,
Then to the hospital to deliver in lamentation.

For I was alone and a little scared,
But then was happy to see police cars paired.

Nothing could go wrong at stop lights,
When I had pains with no plights.

I got to the hospital and all went well,
Then came daddy by cab and he thought it was swell.

Lee gave his daughter the name of Annette,
After the Mickey Mouse Club brunette.

Yvonne fit well thought Marilyn after her much-loved cousin in Kansas.
They enjoyed the new baby as much as any man says.

The maternal grandparents came to California,
To love and see what was born ya.

At a month old, Annette and Marilyn went home
To Indiana to see the rest of the clan.

Lee was soon out of the Navy with no more pays,
And decided in Indiana he wanted to spend the rest of his days.

There was no work in Lafayette,
So we settled in Chicago with a new layette.

Marilyn went back to GMAC,
And Lee went to school for me.

Annette grew to kindergarten age, but welcomed
A little brother at nearly three.

First grade was started at Lafayette,
Where she stayed much of her life thereafter.

Some of her time sent her to Georgia
Where she enjoyed her euphoria.

She found her way back to home,
Never more to roam.

Except on vacation
And much to her elation.

She loves to travel,
And there came to unravel
All her woes.

Her son Owen came later,
And she was a good little mater.

Dave became her soul mate,
And she was elated to be top rate.

Solid, sound, dependable,
And never replaceable.

I always remember you,
As my helpful, grateful, loving daughter
That sees everything through.

I love you, my dear lovely first born,
And will always toot your horn.

 Yours loving mother, Marilyn

"Mothers were once daughters"   by Helen Steiner Rice

(I sent this poem to Annette near her high school graduation and put it in her life album I created for her in May, 1981 upon graduation.

Every home should have a daughter,
For there's nothing like a girl to keep the world in a whirl.

She's a wondrous combination of a mind and brain and heart,
And she contributes so much from the start.

She becomes a sweet girl graduate, a bride then a lovely woman.

And there would be no life at all
Without a darling daughter,
Who in turn, becomes a mother.

Thank you Helen Rice!

"Jeffrey Scott" (My second born)

My second born and only son–
All our hearts you have won.

Just twenty days from your wedding
We in joy are sure betting,
That life will give you happiness.

When you first asked for a brother,
I used to tell you we needed no other.

You were rambunctious and full of energy
Enough for two or three.

You loved to climb trees,
And often skinned your knees.

Stitches were not spared,
For your wounds I always care.

My favorite sight of you,
Was a darling remembrance of you in a stew

You took your grandmother's flour,
And dumped it on your head with power.

With some Irish blood from your father,
I wanted a name that would matter.

I thought Shawn Patrick
Would make a perfect Irish name.

Even Patrick after my Swedish father,
Could show some fame.

Your dad would hear of no such thing,
So we settled together on this name with zing.
Jeffrey Scott fit together, and had a nice ring.

You were destined though to
Love your Swedish heritage,
Maybe I should have given you a Swedish
narrative.

You were born in a Swedish hospital of Chicago,
But you grew up in my home town of Lafayette.

You traveled back to Chicago for college,
And lived all over for knowledge.

You taught, you learned,
And never felt burned.

For life was a stage,
Where you wrote every page.

I see how fine you've grown,
And how far you've come,
And now I'm so proud of who you've become.

You're adventurous and not afraid;
You know how much you've paid.

I'm so proud of who you are,
This man you've become.

May you and Joanna be forever happy,
And enjoy a lovely new life for years to come.

I want it to be known-
That I will love you forever even though you are grown.

 Love you always, your Momma

"Kristina Amelia Elisabeth" (My third born)

(named after her Swedish grandmother on her grandfather's side)

Tina dear, when I lost my third child by design, I wrote a poem along this line.
I felt if it was not to be, then maybe some day all would be glee.

I didn't know if God would send this little being to me later, or if I was to see him or her in heaven along with other loved ones. I lost two more tries at expanding our family before God blessed us with you. Thus, I call you my first "miracle" baby- this precious little girl who worked so hard along with her mother to come into this world to become another life was tough.

After you reached five,
Momma had to go to work so we could survive.

Teenage years were rough,
You rebelled and thought you were tough.

We got through all those tests,
Cause momma tried to know what was best.

I loved you so much, I would hug you,
And tell you so and hoped it would do.

I got through those years, and welcomed a new life for you,
When you married John and said "I do".

You have studied and struggled to get through many years of school;
You carried the ball and expanded your family-that really is cool.

I love you my Tina, named after Kristina,
My grandmother in Sweden, whom none of us have met-
But I'm sure she'd be just as proud of her namesake, you bet!

You chose very early to be called "Tina" even though I preferred "Kristina".

I remember our rocking chair songs when you were a little girl,
And your learning to sing was such a pearl.

Your voice was like a lark,
And it gave me such a spark.

You tried your hand at the organ,
And even a little modeling.

I think you had fun as a child–
Even though it was a little wild.

You increased your family with three beautiful girls,
And they all grew the cute little curls.

Kelsey, Emily and then Corrine came late,
But they had increased our love for your mate.

Your career as a dental hygienist
Has been with several fine dentists.

We love what you bring to the family;
Your smile, your cooking, and your friendship–
It all makes you great and entirely special.

Thank you for being my first miracle baby that we never thought could
happen again.
My precious daughter, you are my friend.

Love your momma Marilyn

"Jennifer, Helen Michelle" (My fourth born)

Another and second baby as a miracle,
Was almost more than lyrical.

We were so lucky at being blessed
By another addition-who would have guessed?

Your big brother wanted a baby brother,
But your sister wanted another-

To keep her company, and you came on her birthday,
So this was perfect so the two of you could play.

A healthy one was wished by parents;
Either sex was very apparent.

We were so blessed to be receiving four;
We would never deplore.

Big brother, Jeff was disappointed at first;
He felt receiving a sister, he was cursed.

As soon as he was allowed to name her,
He already felt better for sure.

Momma picked "Jennifer" and both parents picked "Helen"
For both of her grandmothers.

"Michelle" is the name Jeff picked, after a good friend he had known,
Who had become special to him while feeling alone.

You, dear child, were a baby so fair,
Were lucky to have three names to chose from, but you chose "Jen".

Only one of my girls chose not to nickname herself.

You were very angelic in both looks and demeanor.
You did like to play with your sister, who was only two years older.

Sometimes you were a little "bossy",
But Tina loved you even though you were saucy.

You played and laughed and cried together-
Like two little peas in a pod.

Sometimes you wanted to change your birth dates, so you could have your own.
But later you loved sharing the same birthday, so you wouldn't be alone.

When you became grown,
You would go camping as couples on your birthday in perfect tone.

You always got your own cakes,
For your desires had different takes.

When you grew up without college,
I always knew you would succeed anyway.

You made a success in two businesses you created.
You became a cosmetologist and had a successful nail business.

Then you nailed several title closing jobs,
That hardly anyone can do in a whole mob.

I'm so proud of what you've accomplished.
You're a go-getter and never say "can't".

Sometimes the baby of a family succeeds because her family stands behind her to the end.
Loyalty and faithfulness are important to you,
And your family and friends return them and come through.

Your sweet disposition has been your strength.
You have friends who will stay by you at length.

You may not be a biological mother,
But you have another-Kandace.

May you and Bob always have a wonderful life together.

God bless you sweetie, from your mother with love.

"Cheryl"

Felt like she had always been mine from the start,
In her roll she definitely played the part.

She came to Indiana and then we traveled to California to see her family
of four.

We traveled by train for two days,
Then went to Thousand Oaks other ways.

We visited Gene's brother by car
And our trip we could not bar.

Gene did not want to fly by plane,
So only one more trip we took by same.

Cheri came several times for a visit,
And this was just exquisite.

We settled for burning up telephone wires,
And that had to do instead of tires.

Birthdays and Holidays
And some in between became our ways
To correspond.
Sometimes we relied on email,
Instead of snail mail.

When Papa got sick, Cheri and I many times would talk
She would check in like a hawk.

Her busy schedule and sickness
Prevented her from coming like a thickness.
She felt bad she couldn't come-
But we wanted her to be safe and urged her not to be dumb.

She complied and sent her best,
And we all knew she needed her rest.

I love her so and feel all the time,

That she is as close as if she were mine.
With loving thoughts,
Momma Marilyn

"James" (Gene's son)

I didn't meet Jimmy until he was thirty,
But his dad was my new friend who had become my flirty.

Jimmy was tall and lanky,
Quiet and very spanky.

He was remarkable and swift to learn,
All the fine things his dad taught him-he did not spurn.

He is clever at doing tasks
That many of us only mask.

A good papa is he,
And his girls regard him with glee.

Finishing floors was his profession,
Until he decided to labor by concession.

He's worked on his house also-
To bring it up to par to keep it in tow,

Hours never seem to be plentiful,
So he is striving to balance a plate full.

He loved his dad,
And for this they were always glad.

He keeps contact with his mom and sister,
And always cares as a very kind mister.

Continue to grow and be like your dad,
I guarantee you'll not be sad.

Your loving step-mom, Marilyn

My In-Laws

Dave (My son-in-law)

You are my first-born's hubby,
And we're all blessed, cause there could be no subby.

You're calm, congenial, and dependable,
And we all know you are not expendable.

Your papa had been my childhood friend,
And we were all happy you chose Annette in the end.

You, Dave, have been a wonderful "big brother"
To several young boys who could have no other.

I love your firey red hair,
But you could never use it as a snare.

Your proposal in the costume as a bunny,
Was cute and even a little funny.

You were not so typical, but delightfully traditional-
When you asked for the hand of my daughter without being conditional.

You brought order, warmth, and love-
Into a family like a dove.

Not only are Owen and Annette blessed,
But so are all the rest.

Your special demeanor
Could never be keener.

And I am thrilled to be called
Your momma Marilyn as your mother-in-law.

"Joanna" (My daughter-in-law)

My son waited so long to bring you home,
But it didn't take long before we knew
you belonged.

You fit right in from the start,
And we knew you probably would be a part
of our family.

You went to Purdue University in our fair
town;
We decided to keep you around.

You were so gracious and demure-
You were very lovely and pure.

We have had such fun visiting on all the holidays;
Our time together never had enough days.

Your trademark melt-in-your-mouth sugar cookies
Became our family favorite by experts and rookies.

Your sweet, kind, gentle personality
Make it fun for all as a reality.

I love your precious smile,
And always want you to stay a while.

You have wonderful folks,
Who have similar strokes
As your fine qualities.

They undoubtedly have taught you
Many of the wonderful things you do.

I'm so glad my son
Your heart has won.

You are talented and clever
In your job-such a lever.

Live long, happy and blessed,
And grow in wisdom and get plenty of rest.

Welcome my dear new daughter,
And trust we never will our friendship slaughter.

Sincerely, your loving mother-in-law, momma Marilyn

"John Ethan" (My son-in-law)

You came along early in Tina's life,
And it wasn't long till you made her your wife.

She fell for you hard at an early young age,
And you started to write on her page.

You were high school sweethearts,
And you two determined you'd never part.

Kelsey came soon to increase your joy,
And thereafter followed two more with a ploy.

Frolic there was with much fun-
But never to be was a son.

That's OK, cause dad loves all his girls,
Cause they are cute in all their curls.

Kelsey, Emily, and then came Corrine-
Who always puts everyone in a spin!

He's not only a great dad,
But he makes his Tina glad.

Love is grand even after years of twenty,
And now we hope the years will be more - aplenty.

John works hard all summer,
On the roads - be glad he's not a plumber.

Big trucks take him all over,
And we're glad he's not a mower or a mover.

He first wanted to be a policeman
For the Department of Natural Resources,
But now he's cool by blacktopping the courses.

He's recently been promoted to head of the Teamsters,
So now he sits behind a desk on his keister.

He's kind and gentle,

Always helping others with their rental.

Wherever there's a need,
He always takes heed.

He's a great cook on the grill,
And your tummy he can always fill.

A good guy is he,
And we enjoy his fun side with glee.

> Thanks for being a great son-in-law, John.
> Your loving mother-in-law, Marilyn

"Bob" (My son-in law)

You are last of the sons-in-law to my last daughter,
And I'm glad you caught her.

You have made her so happy-
Especially cause you're a dandy pappy.

She loves your daughter, Kandace,
Just as though she were her own.

Your little family brings joy
To an old grandmother who isn't at all coy.

Helpful and congenial are your actions;
We all benefit from these factions.

The family is honored to have you be a part;
And from any job we know you'd never dart.

Take time every day
To leave kind words or say…
"I love you" to family.

Enjoy your life,
And keep it free from strife.

    Lovingly, from your mother-in-law, Marilyn

Carm, Carmen tis the name of my dear sweet sister-in-law.
From the very first day I met her, I knew we'd be the best of friends.
Unusual was our meeting,
As it was without the presence of my mate.

He dared not fly,
Because he got sick when he took to the sky.

Our domains were so far apart,
But I yearned to meet my new in-laws and take them into my heart.

Their eldest was to marry,
And in our meeting, I did not want to tarry.

Gene had a house in California;
It needed tending to and I needed support.

So together my other real estate sister-in-law, Kathy,
Went with me to help me report.

We took care of business with steam,
And enjoyed a family wedding supreme.

Not wanting to be a burden,
We tried to pitch in and lighten Carm's load.

We laundered, we cleaned and even cooked a bit,
As our first meeting we surely wanted to be a hit.

Who were these strangers who took over her home?
Carm surely thought we should roam.

However, this wonderful lady
Took us in and welcomed us with melody.

I brought a greeting on tape,
From all in the family their well-wishes to make.

Since others couldn't come either,
I wanted to show them their hearts wished to be there.

They hadn't visited each other of late,
So I hoped this video would show no hate.

The Californians came back to Indiana later for many visits,
And their bonds became stronger and longer.

Sisters Ruth, Connie, and Marcia visited many times by plane,
And brother Gene and Marilyn went by train.

I'll never forget how much praise and kindness Jake gave me for taking good
care of his brother—this was a given.
Since we loved each other so much—it was just part of liven.

The years of twenty,
Brought love a plenty.

The sometimes rough exterior of the Grenat Clan,
Was brought to tender love with a plan.

Carmen and Marilyn were the "out-laws" of the bunch,
But gatherings became more than a hunch.

These two girls loved two brothers,
And their love for one another was like no other.

As years came and went, tragedies abounded,
But weddings, fun and even funerals kept them grounded.

Siblings and parents died and we joined together,
And kept our bonds and loyalties to each other.

I'll never forget the final day of my beloved Gene,
When Carmen came out of love and respect—
To be here for me and the family without neglect.

Her presence meant the world to me,
And her lovely eulogy and tribute to Gene was all it needed to be.

Through the years we laughed and we have cried,
But our relationship couldn't be better if we tried.

We gained two brothers and we lost two brothers,
But we have never lost our friendship and love for one another.

As time goes on she reminds me how she thinks I changed the life of my Gene,
But we all know that he could never be mean.

We both will be forever changed and strong.
For having been in the family so long.

Thanks, Carmen dear, for always being there for me.
I'll always love you and be there for thee.

**This photo was taken in Arizona, when Carm came to be
with me for my son's Funeral. It meant so very much.**

Grand Children

"Kelsey" (1st of third born-Tina)

You are my first blood grandchild-what a joy!
My middle daughter had you and it was not a ploy.

She loved you from the start,
And right away we all took part.

A new little girl to love and hold,
You looked so much like Mommy-it was though you had come from a
mold.

Precious and sweet you were most of the time-
But sometimes you'd cry in rhyme.

You made your parents change their clothes a lot-
As you spit up your bottle till you were a tot.

Mommy and Daddy went to college with a toddler in tow,
And you grew so quickly and time didn't go slow.

You lived many places all over the state-
That you had to keep up with their paces.

The boyfriends came and went,
As you grew into a time well spent.

You left behind your doll age,
And then went to grade school, high school and college.

You are today a young woman that I will always be so proud of.

You've become head of HR at two major companies, and
This my sweet dear, is a major accomplishment-oh so grand.

Now we're anticipating the coming of your first baby,
And we all are so excited, and I don't mean just maybe.

Congrats to you and Brett-for this wonderful new start,
That all of us are looking forward to being a part.

Lots of love from Mormor,
(Momo {Grandma} Marilyn)

"Emily" (2nd of my third born-Tina)

You are my second blood grandchild,
You came so sweet on Father's Day;
Your big sister, Kelsey, was happy and gay.

She cried when she had to leave you,
In the hospital that night so blue.

She wanted to just take,
You home and her little sister make.

You were so angelic with bright blue eyes,
And a halo of blond little curls and no cries.

You clung to your Nana Sandy
Without any promise of candy.

You've grown so fast and then to high school,
Then ready to drive-that was cool.

You seemed too young for boyfriends,
But several you've had as life always sends.

After graduation from high school,
Came college with all it's tools.

Your future will be bright,
Cause you've worked with all your might.

Now you're a Mrs. and married to a fine man,
And will do well with him at hand.

Love your Lord and keep Him close every day,
And you will see it will definitely pay.

Your Momo Marilyn loves you to no end,
And this you should know-my support I'll always send.

Love, Momo Marilyn

"Corrine" (Third of third born-Tina)

You are fourth blood grandchild,
And have been like my own.
Although your folks only gave you to me
on loan.

John and Tina are your parents,
But I watched you as a grandparent.

You have so many caring people,
Who love you to the steeple.

Godparents, Julie and Keith,
Are wonderful to the peak.

You have aunts and uncles, cousins and friends-
They all love to give to you with all the new trends.

Never forget all our fun tea parties,
Because we bonded there from the start.

You're spoiled rotten-
But it's our fault-as we all cotton.

We are thrilled to see you this year-
In Kindergarten with new friends so dear.

We've trained and tried to teach you new
letters,
So you could do better and better.

We long for your success
As you go along without stress.

K-12 will pass, then comes college-
For you to grow into fine knowledge.

Momo loves you, this you know
Because she always tells you so.

Love you—love you more—that's always our motto!

Your Momo Marilyn

"Owen" (My firstborn's son-Annette)

You are my third blood grandchild.
My firstborn had you late,
But you're well worth the wait.

Your folks lived in Indiana South,
And it was a joy to hear by mouth.

You were already here,
So come quickly to see my new little dear.

A grandson so precious and sweet;
I knew I would melt at your feet.

The day I held you, I was yours at the start,
And I knew it would be hard to depart.

I've watched you play,
And grow and can only say,
You're a joy at whatever you do.

I love to watch you play ball, succeed in school, go to your dances,
And will love to see you in all of your advances.

You tried college, but didn't care too much for it,
But that's okay, cause you'll find the right fit.

You married your high school sweetheart,
And we think she brings out the best part
Of a wonderful union for you both to have from the start.

May you and Paige have a wonderful marriage.
And some day there may be a baby carriage.

Keep close to your maker all the days of your life,
Then there will be minimal strife.

I love you guys so much,
Your Momo Marilyn (Grandma)

"Kandace" (Bob's daughter)

You are our last grandchild,
By marriage for sure-but oh so sweet and mild.

You are an added extra bonus from Bob,
But we love you a whole gob.

Jenni was not to be a natural mother,
But she doesn't need any other.

You fill her bill and please her so,
That she couldn't be happier-don't you
know.

You were such fun at trying
To make Swedish coffee bread, and we
laughed so hard, we were almost crying.

You fill our homes with joys-
And a friend of Owen's and all the boys.

A grandmother's love and heart
Always has room for every one from the start.

Keep studying and growing,
And remember our Father in Heaven will keep you going.

Family is important and grand,
And we all love you to beat the band.

Keep close to parents, and listen real close,
Cause they will always love you the most.

You never can have too much
In the way of family-just know that that is the right touch.

Remember grandma Marilyn is an extra who loves you too.

"Damiana" (James' daughter & Gene's granddaughter)

This was my very first grandchild, that I acquired through marriage.
That sweet little, tanned, brown-haired girl never caused disparage.

Her small five-year frame,
With happiness she always came.

She was bubbly and cute,
And very rarely mute.

Damiana was happy to be able to see
A grandma that came from by the sea.

And now a new grandma in addition to her other-
She was left with us occasionally by her mother.

We had so much fun,
But she kept us on the run.

Time went fast as she grew and finally married Nate,
And he became a really fine mate.

College and a career helped her learn more responsibility.

Then they found a home where children could be reared,
And one day they filled one of their empty rooms
With melody baby tunes.

Little Ethan was added with all his laughter,
And he has filled their home with more love to the rafters.

Keep God in your lives and grow together in harmony,
A home full of love, is what for you should strive.

Always remember dear,
Grandma loves to keep you near.

　　With love, your grandma Marilyn

"Afton" (James' daughter & Gene's granddaughter)

Eight years after Damiana, came little baby Afton.

Big sister was real handy,
And as a baby sitter, was a dandy!

She protected and watched her
As a good big sister.

Afton liked rabbits and took them to the Four-H fair,
Where many blue ribbons they had won as a pair.

Sissy had taught her many things,
And this we saw by what she brings.

She gave tender care
To kittens, dogs, and bunnies-especially to one caught in a snare.

Big sister again came to her rescue,
When she and gram followed Dami's cue.

Grandparents' day at Dayton, brought grandpa & grandma to school;
Performances and refreshments were always cool.

Sweet and affectionate were Afton's marks.
She crawled into grandpa's lap with sparks.

Time was spent with grandparents during the county fair,
And she and grandma became quite a pair.

Holidays with cousins
Was spent with lots of buzzins.

Portraying Saint Lucia was one of her favorite school events.
She wore her white robe and candles in her hair,
And passed out Lucia buns with no despair.

She even did so at grandma's church,
And never left her in the lurch.

Christmas was fun when we were all together,
And memories will last us all forever.

Graduation had finally come,
And we all look forward to what you will become.

Your loving grandma Marilyn

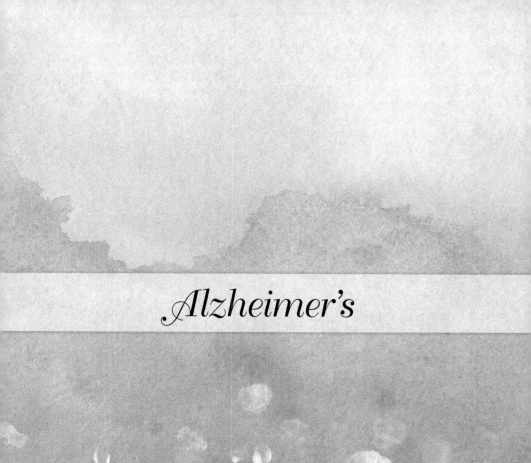

Alzheimer's

"Alzheimer's" by Anonymous & Marilyn March 6, 2018

Don't ask me to remember,
All my memories are a blunder.

Don't try to make me understand,
Just hold my hand.

Do not lose your patience with me,
I can't help the way I'm acting even though good I try to be.

Just know the best of me is gone.
So love me 'til my life is done.

Gene, Gene, the dancing machine;
This is what the kids all called him.
Your mother named you after her father,
And calling you that was not a bother.

So shortening Eugene to Gene,
Became your name with esteem.

You were kind of heart,
And sociable too in part.

Because you were much like your mother,
People said you were like no other.

You were good at sports,
And good in school.

The Air Force took you to ports,
And taught you your tools.

You married young and had two children,
One was Cheri, and othern was Jimmy.
You loved them so till there was no more gimme.

You helped to build the Stealth,
And then it created wealth.

After years of being alone,
You came back to Lafayette all forlorn.

You met your Marilyn wife,
And then with her you spent your life.

Alzheimer's came at a great surprise,
And gave us both a disease of despise.

We'd hoped to try to live our life
Without too much strife.

We love each other and our Lord.
And we know we'll thrive and not be bored.

When you fall into bed at night,
You're so relieved you don't have to fight.

Grab a few winks before
It starts all over with some more.

Some nights are peaceful,
Some are up and down.
But pray you can rest before you feel you'll drown.

Life is not all bad with an Alzheimer's patient who's lame,
For you see, we love them just the same.

Oh those Alzheimer's tangles - it's a horrible disease.
That never gives us any ease.

It messes with the mind,
And always puts us in a bind.

About the time we think we have it figured out —
It gives us another bout.

When the victim can't remember words,
He makes new ones up in blurts.

I've made a new dictionary of his sayings —
That makes no sense to anyone.

He cannot follow instructions,
So he makes all kinds of destructions.

Sometimes he's sorry and shows loving actions,
And all of a sudden he can't stand you and backs off.

Occasionally, he will run away,
And you have to be clever and pretend to play.

Clever you must always be,
As the caregiver, don't you see?

Sometimes he may want to give you a punch —
But you have to be smart a whole bunch.

When it is time to eat, he is usually ready.
But you must hurry and be steady.

After you feed him a plate full —
He may say, "Why haven't you fed me?"

When pill time comes, he may take them or throw them away;
So be smart and figure how to give them to him in a new way.

He may forget your name,
But you have to not give him blame.

Bedtime is another story —
If you want it smooth with glory.

He may fight you for his clothes

And may not want PJ's over his toes.

His shoes may go on opposite feet.
Clothes on top of others makes dressing hard to complete

Since he napped much of the day,
He may not want to hit the hay.

TV confuses his thoughts,
And he thinks it's real situations;
So try to convince him it's just not so.

Be patient and kind,
And then you'll never be behind.

Love is the answer, my friend,
And always give it to the end.

What a brave soul gone in,
To fight the ghoul to win!

The monsters of Alzheimer's try to tear apart the heart and mind.
We know it's miseries are very unkind.

My dear kind, wonderful being
Has been turned into one without reasoning.

He was one so whole, intelligent and gentle,
Who now can not be mental.

We used to laugh, talk, and mince,
And now he is no longer my prince.

I can't help but wonder —
What's in that poor jumbled blunder?

Does he know? Can he think?
Or is he troubled to the brink?

I think he knows I love him so,
But he can't tell me — so I know.

When oh when will there be a cure —
So again I can see him as pure?

He once was so smart —
Now I want this nightmare to depart.

He once helped develop the stealth
That won the Gulf War and brought wealth.

He loved his country and Air Force job,
And never would back down from a mob.

I wrote this little dity-
Not to receive your pity,

But just so you can understand.
Let's get down to business and work to help to beat the band.

All these poor minds wanting to know
Just why this has made such a blow...
      To mankind.

We would love to see it all go away —
To make a new life for the folks to stay.

Please find a cure —
To make them all pure.!!!

"Gene my future"   *May 2, 2011 (one month after his*
death)

While my sweetheart has left me physically,
He has not left me spiritually.

Gene will always live within my heart.
Love does not melt away.
But dwells where it can grow-from within.

Gene is being strengthened for our next life.
God wants wonderful things for him.

He is strong, invincible, everlasting only because God wants him for
His army to conquer all evil.

How did we get here?
We know Gene is the Gentle Giant who can conquer that which we fear,
And do not want present.
My Gene is my hero, my love and God's advocate. May God bless him and
Show him the way to conquer-to acquire by force of arms. Only by His power
And love to empower or give capacity to do good to all mankind.

In our hope for goodness-may we love all of God's people and encourage them
To inspire all peoples to follow God's will.

Our next life will be joyous and we will love each other equally and completely.
My Gene, I love you, I wait for you to return and take me with you to a
new heaven.
We will be together forever as friends and one. We love Him who made us.

By your partner in both lives, lovingly your Marilyn

My Grandpa has Alzheimer's

What is that?

All the time he repeats himself.
Loving us is always natural.
Zero time to settle disputes.
Have a good time with grandchildren.
Every day is different.
I love to help others understand.
Much of the disease is unavoidable.
Even family doesn't always know.
Remember patience, love and
'Soft voices are very important.

We care that our beloved
Must always receive coveted-

Help to enjoy each day
In the fine array.

We give them reprise
With a great surprise.

They love rehashing the past
With a lovely photo album with class.

Memories are brought forth
And they again can have worth.

Don't force them to do what they don't want to
Just give them a chance to live like we should do.

Short-term memory is very difficult
So give them room to get the best result.

They don't always know how wonderful
Life can be with loved ones on hand without being dull.

One day they may know you,
And the next they may dismiss you.

Just give them a chance
To remember and advance.

We want to help them
As best we can as a gem.

Momo's life has been frayed
But she is not afraid.

Grandpa will survive
And we will all have pride.

To give him support
In this time with resort.

He wants to be on the go
And we just let him do so.

Sometimes food can defer him
But sometimes he leaves us grim.

Occasionally police have helped to find our sweet
And this is always such a treat.

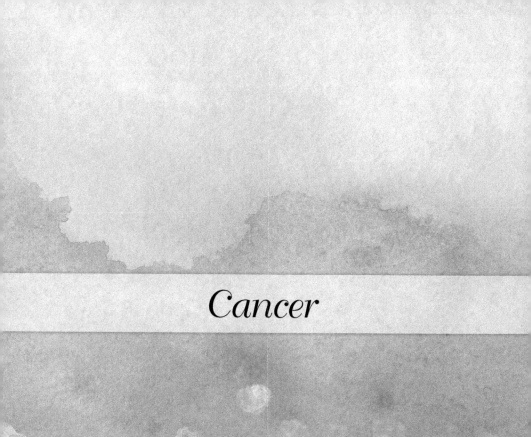

Cancer

"The hue of blue"

I am definitely so blue—
This is a very sad & bad hue.
I heard today an awful dilemma.

It came from my son's Doctor's diagnosis—
The analysis told us a very grim prognosis.

We were very sad of the forecast,
As we hoped the prediction would be good and steadfast.

My son has fought the tough good fight—
Long and hard through many a night.

I mourned with my daughter,
I mourned with my brother, and
I mourned with my Prayer Pals too.

Where else can one go when there's
Nothing less than blue?

Cancer has been our family sin—
How can anyone ever win?

This iniquity has hampered and hurt
Us like nothing else short of dirt.

We have hoped and prayed for a miracle
To make all disaster bettered by the Spiritual.

Please dismiss this agony of pain,
So we no longer need to disdain.

Why oh why do you continue to pursue
So that we have to abstruse?

We just try to understand
What the purpose is at hand.

We only know we must try to do
The best we can to be discerning,
When it comes time to show clever anew.

Please God, remember us as we plea,
So that all the calamities will flee.

Once again our family has been hit
With a doozy of the pits.

Why oh why some may say,
While all the while we try to smile.

God is good we know,
And we try our courage to show,

That we have faith in the Father above,
As our feelings, hurts and doubts we give a shove.

Cancer has reared it's ugly head,
And we so much want it to be dead.

We have it in the colon, prostate, lungs, uterus,
Ovaries, abdomen and breast.
Now you tell us God knows best.

Yes, He does, but trying to make sense
Of this yet another terrible disease as we sit and
Wait on the fence.

There is ovarian, leukemia, melanoma,
Esophageal, mesothelioma, and now lymphoma.

Is there anywhere this horrible man-eater doesn't attack?
We just want to beat her and fight back.

Especially when it has put so many of our family at risk,
We want healing to be most brisk.

History and research has shown many ways to fight this ugly disease,
And it's our turn to wait out this game of cat and mousey.
Why does chemotherapy leave our loved ones feeling so lousy?

The promise of healing comes slowly–
While all the while, the sick feel lowly.

Hair is lost, weight is lost,
And the patient pays the cost.

Cute little hats and wigs
Are worn with their new digs.

Changes in smells, atmosphere, tastes and sounds
All affect the patient in leaps and bounds.

Gaunt looks of despair from little ones to the elder
Haunt the family and friends as they scurry helter skelter.

They are trying to make good food,
And other pleasing things to better their mood.

Small things become large,
And all are trying not to let them become a carnage.

It is hard on family to watch their loved ones suffer,
And they just want desperately to be their buffer.

Thank goodness for research, doctors, nurses, and caregivers
Who try their best to give their all to serve–
At Cancer Centers of America, Mayo Clinics, and others with great nerve.

Without the prayers of many from near and far,
For the young and the old, there would be no healing for our star...

Thank you Lord Jesus, our heavenly Papa, for all you do on our behalf–
For without you, we could not find a reason to smile or even laugh.

We know our lives are in your hand,
And for this we can fell truly grand.

Please bring a real cure–
This are we all very sure.

"Childhood Memories Of My Son"   March 11, 2018

Stroke the memories of days gone by,
Take lots of pictures-just lots and lots, stacked high.

Our children grow so fast-
It's easy to forget the past.

I saw a father today of a two year old
Pat his child lovingly, oh so bold.

As his mother held and rocked and danced with him.
You could tell their love was strong within.

I was moved to tears to see this family love-
And it all fit perfectly like a glove.

I was reminded of my loss recently of my son.
Who was the light of my life and my heart he had won.

We had him too short a time,
And he was taken in his prime.

His mom, sisters, cousins, aunts, uncles and wife,
Felt he had too short a life.

His big sister made a beautiful video
That we all enjoyed at his memorial service.

But I had to come home to watch it again-
To soothe my aching heart and have a little grin.

His life was so full of many happenings,
As he had traveled to 80 countries and experienced many trappings.

He loved to climb and conquered many mountains,
In different places too many to count 'em.

He had many friends
At every bend.

He loved family and life
And was ready with a good joke
That he playfully would poke.
But seldom had strife.

Watching that sweet little boy in church today,
Made me remember our former fun play.

We need to keep good records and pictures,
So we can have a good memorable mixture.

I'm thrilled to be able to go back in time
And now see and treasure all I have in rhyme.

Hug your kids today-
So you can savor your play.

Tell them you love them each day
And make memories that will stay.

Miscellaneous

"I believe" — by Anonymous & Marilyn

"
.

I believe that circumstances may have influenced who we are,
But we are responsible for who we become and what we do.

I believe that either you control your attitude, or it controls you.

I believe that you should always leave loved ones with loving words.
It may be the last time you see or talk to them.

I believe the happiest of people don't necessarily have the best of everything;
They just make the most of everything they have.

"How do you want to be remembered?" by Marilyn

I hope I'm remembered as having <u>walked</u> with God.
In order to do that successfully we need to know how to <u>listen</u> to Him.
So life doesn't become grim.

We need in Him to <u>trust</u>.
This is a definite must.

We need to agree with and <u>obey</u> our Savior;
This we should do without worrying about labor.

We may not understand why,
But He will guide us so we won't cry.

If we confess to God, we walk away from sin,
And our lives are secure in Him.

<u>Don't be</u> remembered for being <u>stingy or antagonistic</u>,
Just rely on God to not make us problematic.

Wake up everyday and say,
"With the help of the Holy Spirit, <u>I am going to walk in your way</u>."

Follow Proverbs 3:5-6 (NIV/Bible) "Trust in the Lord with all your heart and lean not on your own understanding; in all your ways acknowledge Him, and he will make your paths straight.

"On hearing classical jewels"   *July 17, 2011*

The sweet music of beautiful sounds,
Pierce my heart, mind and soul that give me grounds
To, of course, put all at rest,
So we can feel our best.

Work all day-
Then we feel we can play.

Please bring me a glass of wine-
Perhaps a long rest to unwind.

Or just sit a spell-
Until the truth we tell,

It's the relaxation of chords
That present themselves in hoards.

We can feel so much better
By following the notes to the letter.

Another elevation for your mind to advance
For a serene existence by chance.

After the end of a busy day,
May all your woes go away.

Calm your nerves, play your tunes,
Lift your spirits to soar with the loons.

Sweet classical musical jewels
Soothe the soul as it rules.

"Sweet, sweet home" *July 17, 2011*

Sometimes we think a home has four walls,
But we all know it's the folks within that create the halls.

Memories of home
Help us not want to roam.

We remember mothers, fathers
And siblings that don't bother us.

Enjoyment of holiday dinners
Make us all winners.

Birthday parties for the kiddies-
Where we sing the little ditties.

The warmth of the hearth
Makes us happy from the start.

Warm cinnamony delicious bread baking
Fills our nostrils that mom is making.

Familiar musical tunes playing,
Remind us of why we are staying.

Cheery smiling faces
Fill the table's places.

We gather together to remember
All the wonderful activities from January to December.

We love remembering our family fun
That all of us share as one.

Don't forget to get together often,
And share before you go to your coffin.
It comes all too fast.

Love from your momma Marilyn

"Our family members leave us" September 11, 2010

Our siblings can be first to leave.
They go off to college, service or start careers.
Sometimes they leave to marry and rear little mirrors.

Occasionally we ourselves leave the family to do the same.
Our parents one at a time, are taken, but not to blame.

The Lord on high had need of him or her,
While the rest of us are left in a blur.

Life continues in each new family formed.
We all get so busy,
We don't seem to have time for each other any more.

Children also leave the nest;
They just want to try to do their best.

As all families expand,
They also at one point disband.

Distances become greater by miles and hurts,
Because sometimes our words become blurts.

Written or spoken words may be hard,
And we can't take back that which has marred.

If we do, it doesn't charm;
They have already caused the harm.

Sorry, sorry, sorry
Means nothing to some,
One can plead till the tears come.

Separation comes in many forms,
To family members who only want unity instead of mourns.

So take each member to your heart today
To your Father God in heaven without delay,
And pray that all your differences are righted this way.

That we no longer carry grudges to our grave some day.

If you are alone today and feel the squeezes,
Thank the Lord for our friend, Jesus.

(I wrote this one day when I felt my brother had left me in heart,
And I felt very despondent in part.

We hurt each other with words,
And my heart was broken in herds.

I'm happy to say we mended bridges,
So now there are no ridges.

I love you Ralph with all my heart; always have, and always will!)

Listen to me dear child-
I gave you a great gift-LIFE,
But God gave you a greater gift-ETERNAL LIFE!

Don't waste this one without trying-
To grow and become something special without crying.

You can be proud to help others-
This would please all mothers.

You can be happy to cure incurable diseases,
Or perform in great releases.

You will be praised to choose a magnificent mate-
And then to rear children not to hate.

Teach them good manners, courtesy, and respect,
And all mankind will give them no neglect.

God's love must be taught through scripture
In a Bible-based church with a mixture

Of action and belief to give relief
To a family of many peoples who want no grief.

We must love all our neighbors
Just as ourselves without labors.

Help the poor, the orphan, and help the widow,
This, dear ones, is a message to which I can say 'ditto'.

The Bible instructs us to love and forgive our enemies-
As we struggle to make sense of these.

We need to honor and obey our Lord and parents,
Just because pleasing God is apparent.

Be patient and kind and peacemakers
To all mankind-even the takers.

Do not be proud, loud, or stay in a cloud.
Do not be rude, crude, or be a bad dude.

You will win favor with man,
If you keep your name the best in the land.

Be reliable, faithful and true
In your friendships, work, relationships, and stick like glue.

Trust the Lord as your stronghold,
Even though we wear a blindfold.

Remember Christ Jesus died for us to have eternal life,
And this I know, because he did it with lots of strife.

Forgive others, even though they may not forgive you,
And do not always worry about giving them their due.

Take care of family members always,
Just to show them love on all highways.

Read your Bible every day and pray,
And let folks say-you're okay.

Listen to me dear little ones as I rave-
There's just one thing I want you to know-
I love each of you just as though-
You were the only child I have.

Even the ones I lost
At a terrible cost.

All my babes in a row,
Are Annette, Jeff, Shawn, Mical, Lauren, Tina, and Jen-
And they I gladly would take in tow.
Now I've claimed them all by pen.

"The Desperate Sufferance of a Man's Children" February 23, 2018

How can this be?
A cruelty for many to see?

Yes, this man who was loved by many
But left his own children without any.

How could he be so unaware to not see–
What all knew he needed to be?

His wife worked hard at two jobs and sometimes three–
To make a good life as best she could give thee.

They were rejected and left in despair–
When all they wanted was love and attention to spare.

He promised to come and get the children for an outing,
But left them desiring and ending up pouting.

Isn't that a form of child abuse of sorts?
And we see it in all the reports.

Children were reared anyway in a caring environment by their mother–
Hoping always to give them love without smother.

While fathers are needed
It also is conceded
That mothers try their best
To always give and teach the rest that they should be blessed.

The best they shall have, full of love,
And special nurturing with a kid glove.

Mommas do the best they can
But it's always best with a Daddy too at hand.

So try to do as God intended to keep
family together so family ties you can reap.

It seems in the end
That Fathers can send

Their love and give them the attention–
That should be without mention.

"The perfect jewel found"

Joel found a jewel in a jewelry store.
He could not expect any more.

Ralph found his sweet miss
When he walked into an office of an optometrist.

Who knew finding a mate
Would be better than fate.

My prince I discovered through a high school reunion,
And we had a perfect union.

How did you find your true love?
Do you feel they were sent from above?

God has a plan for each of us,
And if you follow His will, He will give you a plus.

We each can have a blessing
So long as we don't make a messing.

Sometimes our soul mates
Can appear at phenomenal rates.

If you've found him or her,
You can truly concur.

Your jewel can be found almost anywhere,
And we rejoice when we unite the perfect pair.

So keep your eyes open, your heart open,
And be prepared -even if it means elopin'!

Josh, you just keep inspiring me
To write more poems, now this is for thee.

You have such love for your Mother,
Even though she lives farther away than any other.

Your sister you've cared for,
But now have watched her fly away to achieve her own lore.

Grandma lives close by,
So can easily make you a breakfast pie.

You take her to church and enjoy a morn together,
And are usually faithful in all kinds of weather.

She helped you grow into the fine man you are,
And brought the Love of your Savior
To your heart with much flavor.

I'm inspired by your love of family,
And to me always helping with formality.

Because of your patience, guidance and care,
I will always remember you with flare.

Thank you my friend,
I will always appreciate you to the end.

"Momo's Excitement"

Who knows the meaning of this word?
Be happy and fly like a bird.

When you hear you're going to be a great grandma,
You jump for joy and try to demand.

Time to think and digest
All the plans to invest.

The future for the family-
To enjoy time together namely.

Grandma and grandpa can hardly contain themselves.
They are thrilled to think they will be resolved

To help spoil and love this new little one
That will come into all our lives that is spun.

If grandmas can love and have fun,
Think how much more great grandmas will have under the sun.

She or he will be loved so very much,
And all of us will bring our special touch.

Aunts and uncles and even friends
Will come to give without offends.

Some day there will be cousins,
And then the little ones will be buzzin.

New little ones are such a joy,
And we are elated to anticipate your deploy.

Our time of excitement
Will be enhanced with enticement
Of love and giggles from a sweet new surprise moment.

We've recently learned it is a little boy-
Oh, my land, what a great joy.

We will have so much fun,
And a new story will have to be spun.

Momo will love every moment of play,
And we will enjoy all there is to display.

Hope for the morrow,
And new things to borrow.

We will all enjoy the day
That we can all portray.

A memorable time is coming,
And we all will be forthcoming
To enjoy, record and it will be becoming.

See what we have to look forward to-
A blissful, caring, memorable time of definitely not a state of platitude.

A little male will keep and bring much joy,
Excitement, new horizons as only from a boy.

A great grandson will keep us all hopping and wanting to peep,
Into his life always wanting to creep.
In the future to bring a heap
Of love, caring and understanding so deep.

"Love my work, cause it doesn't feel like work" January 1, 2014

Oh Lord, I just came home from work;
I have been blessed with many perks.

I love this job every day,
And I'm lucky enough to receive pay.

My little charges and older folks
Always need all my pokes.

I take care of little ones as a nanny,
And my older folks are very canny.

I hope they love me
As much as can be.

For I love them so much-
As much as a whole bunch.

I count my blessings all the time,
As each day brings new challenges in prime.

The Lord knows who needs me, so He gives me health and strength-
So I can give my best at great length.

I give the best care through my Caregiver Services,
And strive to please all so no one is nervous.

We're living in peace,
Because our Heavenly Father loves us without cease.

I love my clients with loving care,
And no one can dissuade me - not even a bear.

Daily cleaning, washing, and cooking;
I'm always ready for another booking.

Call me, as I'm always ready-
So make me your favorite steady.

"The Caregiver and the client"   *April 26, 2018*

My clients are so special to me;
They make me as happy as can be.

Each day they wait and depend on my assistance,
While all the while there is no resistance.

I do for them as they request,
Always trying to do my best.

They need for me to fetch and carry,
And I never want to tarry.

They need groceries, necessities, and booties;
And I love to appease their desired duties.

They have appointments to meet,
And I love to march to their beat.

Doctors, friends, and hairdressers they want to see,
And to please, I will always take thee.

They may have cleaning or cooking needs,
So I always try to keep them up to speed.

Laundry is always a must,
And this I do with their trust.

We laugh, we talk,
And even sometimes walk.

The elderly or infirmed just need to be
Acknowledged and loved - don't you see.

Take time to provide
So all can abide
In perfect harmony.

"The spirit leads me"

I Corinthians twelve
Teaches us where we should delve.

We each have special gifts
And to us they give substantial lifts.

God has put us here
And it's all very clear.

The Holy Spirit has purpose for us
And to that we should realize
That in the end it's a real prize.

Both for us giving
And to the person living

To receive and be blessed
By all the best

God and we have to offer.

While we knowledge receive,
Of where God wants us, we must believe

That it is Him to all glory be given.
That is the reason for our liven.

The Holy Spirit was given to direct us,
And by His guiding, it's a plus.

Lord, make me pure in heart–
Never from you to depart.

"A True Friend"

A true friend he always is
And I have no doubt to wonder about.

He is special in all he does.
He cares for his Mom,
And that's never a bomb.

When I need him,
He is always at the brim.

He comes to assist,
And I never need to insist.

No matter how small or large the task,
He comes along without a mask.

He covers all the problems
That he can sufficiently solve them.

If I need roofing, electronics, or a picture hanging,
He is there with banging.

A hammer or a drill-
He always comes with skill.

My friend Don is always golden
With much expertise he is bold in.

It's nice to have a friend
That in which we can always depend.

Thanks to the reliable friend
We can always count on in the end.

"Gene's partial eulogy"

After the twenty great years God gave Gene and me, I felt I needed to give his eulogy.

I won't recite the whole thing, but one of the things I mentioned toward the end was this.

That I believe that the more we know about the afterlife, the easier it will be to make the trip when our turn arrives. Freedom from fear generally is the fruit of knowledge. God's perfect love drives out fear. Ignorance can promote fear and even prolong grief after a loss. It can even leave us unprepared for our own death. I have recently been reading a wonderful book by John Burke called, "Imagine Heaven" about folks experiencing Near Death Experiences. I have learned so much from this and been thrilled to hear of doctors and other medical folks coming to the Lord because of what their patients have told them in their NDEs.

There are only two things that really matter during your life on earth.

1) 1) Your relationship with God.
2) 2) And how well you demonstrate your love.

Everything else is meaningless. If you've ever experienced this, you place greater importance on loving others and living each moment for God. Gene always inspired me to do both and he helped me to try to be a better person by example.

Your loving wife, Marilyn
Rest in Peace my dear. YOU HAVE GONE FULL CIRCLE." (This is on his Tombstone.) He always took the long way around too in life.

"Jeff's partial eulogy"

Jeffrey Scott Fleeger battled a rare lymphoma cancer for over three years. He always loved climbing and even conquered Kilimanjaro. He climbed his last peak to meet with our Lord on November 26, 2016. We felt he was too young to go at fifty.

He was married to his lovely wife Joanna and they lived in Tucson, Arizona.

He had traveled abroad to over eighty countries as a travel director while operating his own travel consulting company, Eventures, Inc., for over 20 years.

He also had taught english as a second language to post high school students in Finland for over a year.

While celebrating his life with friends, some of his college buddies from North Park University came to pay their respects in Tucson. His sister, Annette, put together a fun video commemorating many of his feats and accomplishments.

His ashes were fittingly strewn from atop a mountain overlooking Tucson.

His family continues to miss him every day. Rest in Peace my dear Jeff. We shall meet again some day in glory land.

Your loving mother, Marilyn

(I created this last poem to be read at my funeral when the time comes.) Jen said she would read it.

"Marilyn's last letter to my family & friends" August 13, 2012

Death is a time of sleeping,
And those who leave are in God's keeping.

For life is God's promised goal,
And sunshine for the soul.

You must doubt Him never,
As through death man lives forever.

I am not afraid to go-
Even though the exact path I do not know.

He has brought me here,
So I do not fear.

To go with Him to the unknown,
I know I will not be alone.

He will take my hand
As I journey to the promised land.

I will go through the open door
To God's mansion and live for evermore.

Please for me do not shed wild tears,
Or carry sorrow through the years,

I have not been afraid to die,
Cause I know my loved ones who've gone before and those
Who follow will meet me again in the sky.

See you there those I love!

Love, Mom and Marilyn

I too, my dear Gene, have jumped the hurdle, and "Have Gone Full Circle"

The End

Notes

Notes

Notes

Notes

Printed in the United States
By Bookmasters